Past and Present

PLANES

Neil Morris

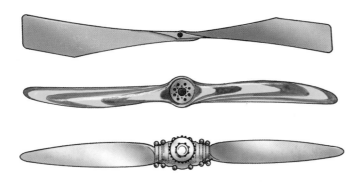

Thameside Press

US publication copyright © 2002 Thameside Press.
International copyright reserved in all countries. No part
of this book may be reproduced in any form without
written permission from the publisher.

Distributed in the United States by
Smart Apple Media
1980 Lookout Drive
North Mankato, MN 56003

Text copyright © Neil Morris

ISBN 1-931983-35-6

Library of Congress Control Number 2002 141367

Printed by South Seas International Press Ltd., Hong Kong

Editor: Honor Head
Designer: Helen James
Picture researcher: Juliet Duff

Words in **bold** appear in the glossary on pages 30–31

Picture acknowledgements:
t=top; b=bottom; c=center

Arcaid: 29b Dennis Gilbert
The Aviation Picture Library: front cover, 12, 16t, 20t, 24t, 25b, 29c
British Airports Authority, Heathrow: 17t
British Airways: 5b
Mary Evans Picture Library: 8 (both), 9, 17c
Hulton Getty Picture Collection Ltd: 13b, 16c and b
Retrograph Archive Ltd: 5t
Rolls Royce PLC: 21
Science Photo Library: 20b NASA, 24b Pat and Tom Leeson
TRH Pictures: 4, 13t US Navy Curtiss, 17b NASA, 25t Westinghouse, 28b Gulfstream
Virgin Atlantic: 29t
Zefa: 28t

Front cover and main artworks by Terry Hadler
All other artworks by Graham Rosewarne

Contents

Introduction

People dreamed of flying thousands of years before the first planes took off. The ancient Greeks told stories of people putting on homemade wings. And the ancient Chinese flew kites.

▼

First flyers

The first machines to take people into the air were balloons. Then inventors built **gliders**. At the start of the twentieth century, engines were added to gliding aircraft. The first powered airplane took to the sky in 1903.

ALA LITTORIA S.A.
ROMA
SERVIZI AEREI

◄ On this 1940s poster, an Italian family are looking forward to their journey on a plane.

Bigger and faster

In the 1950s, **jet engines** changed air travel forever. Planes got bigger, faster, and more comfortable. Later, **jumbo jets** carried more people and flew further. Today, business travelers and vacationers head for the nearest airport for many of their long journeys.

► A jumbo jet flies high over the mountains.

Pioneers of flight

In the early nineteenth century, adventurous people were already flying in balloons and gliders. Then, around 1850, engineers started building flying machines that were powered by steam engines.

The Wright brothers' *Flyer* had a small gasoline engine. This turned two **propellers** behind the wings. The pilot lay on the bottom wing.

Early attempts

Full-sized steam planes were very heavy. Gasoline engines were lighter and more powerful. In 1903, Samuel Langley, an American scientist, launched his plane from a houseboat on a river. But his attempts ended with a damaged plane and a wet pilot!

The Wright brothers

Later the same year, two American brothers made the world's first successful powered flights in an airplane. Orville and Wilbur Wright, who were bicycle makers, used bike chains to attach an engine to the propellers of their plane. On December 17, 1903, in North Carolina, Wilbur made a flight that lasted 59 seconds and covered 870 ft.

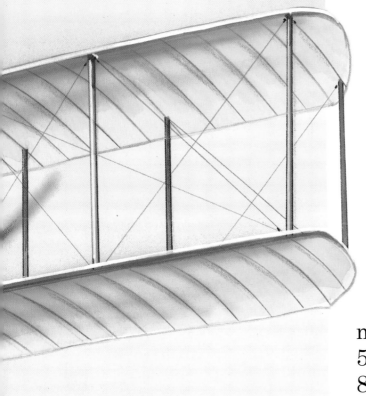

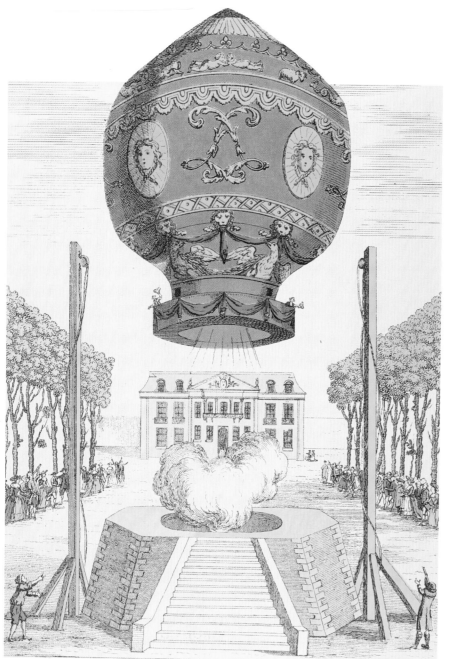

▼ Otto Lilienthal, a German engineer, made more than 2,000 flights with his own gliders. This attempt in 1894 obviously failed!

▲ In 1783, two Frenchmen became the first humans to fly above the Earth. They rose 300 ft over Paris in a hot-air balloon and stayed up in the air for 25 minutes.

Steering
The pilot moved the wings by pulling wires.

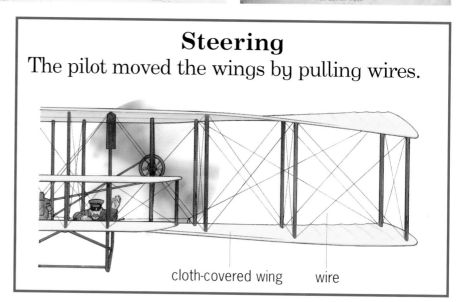

cloth-covered wing   wire

How a plane flies

Propellers push the plane forward, creating **thrust**. This overcomes the **drag** of the air.

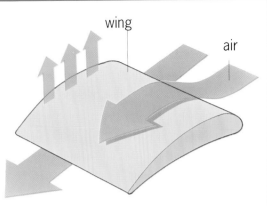

wing

air

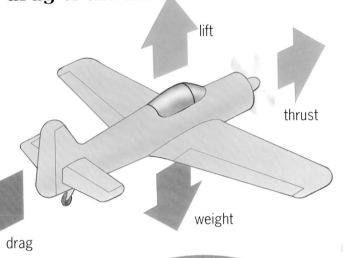

lift

thrust

weight

drag

Taking off

A wing's upper side is curved. Air flowing underneath the flat side pushes the wing up. This creates **lift** to overcome the plane's weight and helps the plane to take off.

◄ In 1909, a French pilot named Louis Blériot flew across the Channel from France to England. This was the world's first international flight. Blériot's plane had a motorcycle engine.

Crossing the Atlantic

Early planes were flown for fun. They were not big enough to carry passengers. Then another use was found for planes — war. During the First World War, from 1914 to 1918, planes became faster and more powerful.

Alcock and Brown flew in an open **cockpit**. Brown had to climb onto the wing to clear ice from the engines.

Alcock and Brown
When the war ended in 1918, a newspaper offered a prize to the first person to fly non-stop across the Atlantic Ocean. It was won by two English flyers, John Alcock and Arthur Brown. They took off from the North American coast of Newfoundland. Sixteen and a half hours later, they landed in Ireland.

Early passengers
In 1919, the first international airline service flew four passengers from London to Paris. In those days, most passenger planes were converted war bombers. Passengers wore leather coats to protect them from the cold, as well as **goggles** and gloves.

Flying in an open cockpit

Alcock and Brown crossed the Atlantic in a converted bomber called a Vickers Vimy. Later in 1919, two Australian brothers flew halfway around the world in the open cockpit of another Vimy. Ross and Keith Smith took 29 days to fly over 10,500 miles from London to Australia, with many stops on the way.

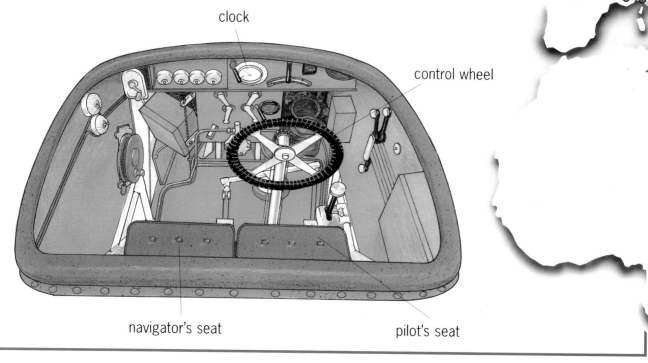

clock

control wheel

navigator's seat

pilot's seat

London

▶ A modern **replica** of a German First World War fighter. This single-propeller plane had a top speed of 90 miles per hour. It had one pair of wings, while many others at the time had two pairs.

▲ This flying boat also flew across the Atlantic in 1919. But it landed on the ocean several times on the way.

Propellers

A plane's propeller is driven by its engine. Metal and wooden propellers changed rapidly between 1909 and 1928.

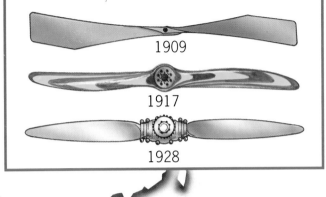

1909

1917

1928

Darwin, Australia

▲ In 1927, the American pilot Charles Lindbergh became the first person to fly solo across the Atlantic.

Air passengers

During the 1930s, companies made planes specially for carrying passengers. Airlines wanted to offer a service that would compete with trains and ships. One of the first aircraft companies was Boeing. In 1933, it launched the Boeing 247.

The all-metal Boeing 247 had a **cruising speed** of 190 miles per hour. Seventy-five of these planes were built.

New design

The **streamlined** Boeing 247 could carry ten passengers. They traveled in a comfortable, heated cabin and could fly right across the United States in less than a day. William Boeing's company went on to become the world's biggest aircraft manufacturer.

Flying boats

There were not many airports outside the U.S. in the 1930s. Flying boats helped overcome this problem. These big planes had a fat **fuselage** and floats under the wings, so they could land and take off on water. Passengers were taken ashore by boat.

► The Douglas DC-3 first went into service in 1936. It had two pilots and a stewardess to look after the passengers. More than 12,000 DC-3s were built, and some are still flying.

◄▲ The German airship, *Hindenburg*, was 815 ft long. On May 3, 1937 it burst into flames in New Jersey, killing 36 people.

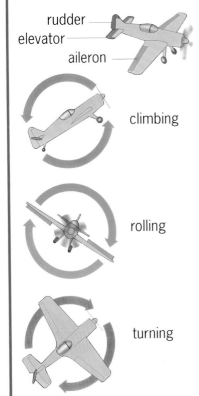

Plane controls
Elevators make a plane climb. **Ailerons** make it roll. A **rudder** turns the plane.

rudder
elevator
aileron

climbing

rolling

turning

▲ These passengers are walking to their plane at an airport near London, England, in 1946. Then, airport buildings were huts and tents.

◄ Passengers began to enjoy in-flight service in the 1930s. Luggage racks were simple nets.

► In 1938, the smaller seaplane took off on the back of the big flying boat.

Jet planes

Before the Second World War, which lasted from **1939** to **1945**, all planes were driven by propellers. Then the jet engine was invented, and this meant that planes could fly much faster.

The German Messerschmitt Me 262 first flew in 1942. This fast plane was powered by two jet engines.

Race against time

British **engineer** Frank Whittle built the first jet engine in 1935, but it was not fitted to a warplane until 1941. German scientists were also working on jet engines, and their jet planes took to the air first. But the early jet aircraft had little effect on the war.

Long-distance travel

Big propeller-driven planes were also built during the war, to carry military equipment and troops. Some of these were used as passenger aircraft straight after the war. By 1950, propeller-driven airliners could carry 100 passengers non-stop from the U.S. to Europe at almost 310 miles per hour.

► The British Gloster Meteor E28/39 was powered by a single jet engine designed by Sir Frank Whittle.

Later Meteors had two jet engines and broke the world air speed record.

▲ In 1947, the American Bell X-I became the first plane to fly faster than the speed of sound. It was carried into the air by a big B-29 bomber. Then it flew off to reach a speed of 672 miles per hour.

Jet engines

A jet sucks in air at the front. A compressor squeezes the air into a combustion chamber, where it is mixed with burning fuel. Burning gases are blasted out at the back. As the gases shoot backwards, the aircraft is pushed forwards.

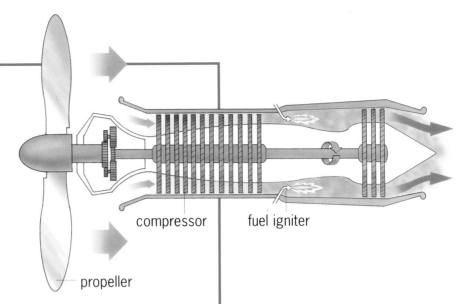

compressor   fuel igniter

propeller

A jet engine with a propeller at the front is called a turboprop.

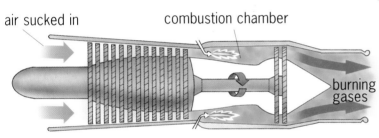

air sucked in   combustion chamber

burning gases

The turbojet is the simplest form of jet engine.

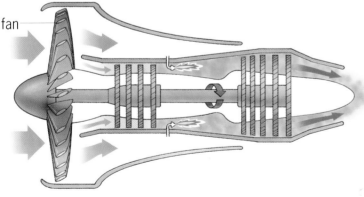

fan

A turbofan engine has a big fan at the front, which sucks in air.

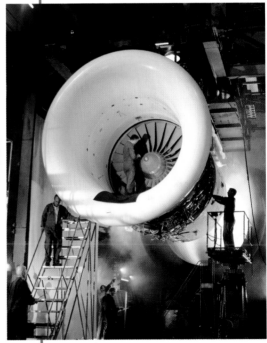

▲ Engineers are checking this huge turbofan engine. Most of today's airliners are powered by turbofans, which are quieter than other jet engines.

World airliners

New jet airliners were built during the 1950s. They made long flights quicker and more comfortable. Bigger airports were built to take them, as new routes opened up all over the world.

The de Havilland Comet was the world's first jet airliner. It had four turbojet engines built into the wings.

Winning passengers

The Comet started flying in 1952. It was much faster and more comfortable than earlier airliners. When jet airliners started flying across the Atlantic, many more people traveled by plane than by ship. Now passengers could travel between Europe and North America in hours rather than days.

Bigger jets take off

Between 1952 and 1954, Comets were involved in a series of crashes. The plane was taken out of service for four years. A new, bigger Comet took to the air in 1958. In the same year, the Boeing 707 started flying across the Atlantic. This big jet plane could carry 179 passengers, many more than the Comet. Later models could fly more than 5,600 miles without landing to refuel.

► In 1954, this Comet was tested to find out why others had crashed. It was found that cracks appeared in the plane's body, caused by a problem known as **metal fatigue**. New aircraft were built with strengthened bodies.

► A modern jumbo jet being built at the American Boeing factory. Every new aircraft is fully tested before it is put into passenger service. New types of planes are first flown by test pilots, who check that they are safe to fly.

Boeing jet airliners

The Boeing 707 began test flights in 1954 and went into service four years later. It was the first of a series of Boeing jet airliners.

Boeing 707

First flew 1954
Length 155 ft
Engines 4 turbojets

Speed 630 mph
Wingspan 148 ft
Passengers 219

◄ **Controllers** on the ground watch **radar screens**. They use radio to talk to pilots in the air.

▼ The 747 is the biggest Boeing. Unlike other airliners, it has passenger seating upstairs.

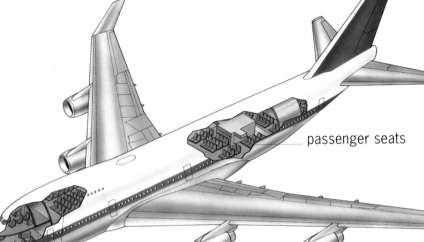

passenger seats

flight deck

passenger seats

► Many of the biggest jet airliners have rows of ten seats across the passenger compartment. These are called wide-body planes.

Boeing 727

First flew 1963
Length 155 ft
Engines 3 turbofans

Speed 625 mph
Wingspan 110 ft
Passengers 189

Boeing 737

First flew 1967
Length 111 ft
Engines 2 turbofans

Speed 567 mph
Wingspan 96 ft
Passengers 149

Modern air travel

Today, there are all sorts of passenger planes, from small executive jets to huge airliners. One airliner, Concorde, can fly at twice the speed of sound.

Concorde is 207 ft long, with a narrow wingspan of 85 ft. It is powered by four turbojet engines.

Jumbo jets

The biggest airliner of all went into service in 1970. This was the Boeing 747, which soon became known as a jumbo jet. This enormous plane can carry as many as 600 passengers. Many other wide-body jets have been built since the 1970s, and these are used for most long flights.

Speed and comfort

Modern air travel is fast and comfortable. Airports have grown bigger, so that they can handle more passengers quickly and safely. But the skies are very busy too, and there are noise problems around many airports. Aircraft have developed over a hundred years from tiny flying machines to huge jumbo jets. How will planes develop over the next century?

► The captain and first officer sit at the controls of a Concorde. The flight engineer sits behind them. The flight deck is covered with instruments.

Boeing 747

First flew 1969
Length 236 ft
Engines 4 turbofans

Speed 613 mph
Wingspan 199 ft
Passengers 516

Boeing 757

First flew 1982
Length 158 ft
Engines 2 turbofans

Speed 571 mph
Wingspan 127 ft
Passengers 239

► Inside the luxurious cabin of a Gulfstream **executive jet**. It is designed so that a small number of people can work and relax during the flight.

◄ Personal video screens make air travel more fun for many people. Passengers choose the movie they want to watch, or they can play computer games.

Boeing 767

First flew 1982
Length 162 ft
Engines 2 turbofans

Speed 562 mph
Wingspan 159 ft
Passengers 242

Boeing 777

First flew 1995
Length 212 ft
Engines 2 turbofans

Speed 578 mph
Wingspan 203 ft
Passengers 440

◄ Young passengers wait for their flight at Kansai Airport, Japan. It is on a man-made island off the coast. The airport can handle 25 million passengers each year.

Glossary

aileron A flap on a plane's wing that is turned to make the wing go up or down.

cockpit The compartment at the front of a plane where the pilot sits.

controller A person on the ground who gives instructions to pilots.

cruising speed The normal speed at which a plane flies.

drag The force of air resistance that tries to hold a plane back.

elevator A flap on the tail of a plane that is turned to make the plane go up or down.

engineer A person who designs and builds planes and other machines.

executive jet A small private jet plane used by business people.

flight deck The compartment at the front of a plane where the captain, first officer, and flight engineer sit.

fuselage The main body of a plane.

glider A plane without an engine.

goggles A pair of glasses for protecting the eyes.

jet engine An engine that helps a plane fly by sending out a jet of hot gases.

jumbo jet A large jet airliner that can carry hundreds of passengers.

lift The force that pushes a plane up into the air.

metal fatigue A weakness that eventually leads to cracks in metal.

propeller A set of turning blades that help a plane to fly.

radar screen A monitor that uses radio waves to show where planes are.

replica An exact copy.

rudder A flap on the tail of a plane that is turned to make the plane turn in the air.

streamlined With a smooth shape to move easily through the air.

thrust The force that pushes a plane through the air.

Index